W9-BNU-240

ALL ABOUT
Coding Loops

BY JAMES BOW

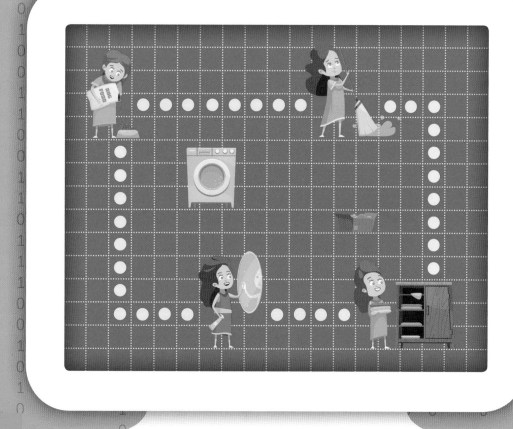

The Child's World®
childsworld.com

Published by The Child's World®
1980 Lookout Drive • Mankato, MN 56003-1705
800-599-READ • www.childsworld.com

Photographs ©: Shutterstock Images, cover,
1, 7, 9, 13, 15, 19, 21, 24; Photos.com/
Getty Images Plus, 5; iStockphoto, 11, 16

Copyright ©2020 by The Child's World®
All rights reserved. No part of this book may be
reproduced or utilized in any form or by any means
without written permission from the publisher.

ISBN 9781503831988
LCCN 2018962819

Printed in the United States of America
PA02418

ABOUT THE AUTHOR

James Bow is the author of
more than 60 nonfiction books
for children. He is a graduate
of the University of Waterloo
in Ontario, Canada, and is a
freelance writer, editor, and
Web designer. He currently
lives outside Toronto with his
wife and two daughters.

TABLE OF CONTENTS

CHAPTER 1

What Are Loops?

Michelle's room is a mess. Her dad tells her to pick up her toys. Michelle picks up one toy and then another until there are no more toys left on the floor. He then tells her to put away her clothes. Michelle neatly folds every shirt and pair of pants until all of the clothes are in the dresser. Her dad then tells her to vacuum the floor. Michelle runs the vacuum back and forth until she has vacuumed the whole floor. Now Michelle's room is perfectly clean!

Michelle repeats the action of folding laundry.

When her dad gave her a command, Michelle cleaned until the job was all done. Michelle cleaned in a **loop**. A loop is when you repeat an action until a job is finished. Computers also use loops to repeat actions.

CLEANING IN A LOOP

Here is what Michelle's actions look like in a loop.

Dad tells Michelle to clean her room.

Are there any toys left on the floor?

No
False

Yes | True

Michelle picks up the toys.

Michelle stops cleaning.

CHAPTER 2

Loops in Code

Loops are an important part of computer **code**. Code is a list of instructions that tell a computer what to do. Computers must be told what to do for every step of a program. Sometimes computers need to repeat certain steps. **Coders** do not want to waste time writing the same steps over and over. So they use loops. Loops tell a computer to repeat a set of steps until a task is complete.

For example, a coder wants a computer to type "Hello" 100 times. The coder writes the instructions for the computer to type "Hello." If the coder uses a loop, she only has to write the instructions once instead of 100 times.

Loops save coders time and make coding easier.

9

CHAPTER 3

Parts of a Loop

Loops have four parts. The first part is the **setup**. This is the code that tells the computer that a loop is about to begin. The setup is followed by a **condition**. The condition sets the rules of the loop. The condition in the earlier example was that "Hello" must be typed 100 times. The condition asks a question, such as, "Are there any hellos left to type?" The answer to the question decides whether the computer enters the loop. If the answer is yes, then the condition is true. If the condition is true, then the computer enters the loop.

The computer asks itself whether a condition is true or false before it enters a loop.

When the computer enters the loop, it moves into the **body**. The body is code that the computer follows when it is in the loop. This is the code that makes the computer type "Hello." The fourth part of a loop is the **increment**. It tells the computer that it has gone through the loop. Every time the computer types "Hello," the increment keeps track. Without an increment, the computer would get stuck in the loop forever.

After the computer has gone through the loop, the loop asks the question again. The computer continues to loop until all of the hellos have been typed. Then the computer leaves the loop. The computer has completed its task.

```
for (setup; condition; increment) {
    body_code
}
```

In the example above, the *for* shows that the loop is about to start. The setup, condition, and increment all go inside parentheses. The code between the curly braces is the body.

CHAPTER 4

Types of Loops

There are different types of loops. Three types of loops are *for*, *until*, and *while* loops. A *for* loop sets how many times the computer needs to go through the loop at the beginning. A *for* loop would tell a computer to go through the loop 100 times so that it types "Hello" 100 times. *For* loops are helpful if the coder knows how many times the computer needs to repeat an action.

```
t dij(int s){

    for(int i =0; i<cnt; i++)
    {
        D[i] = 12001;
    }
    memset(P,-1,600*sizeof(int));
    memset(V,-1,600*sizeof(int));
    P[s] = s;
    D[s] = 0;
    int add = s;
    for(int k =0; k<cnt; k++){
        int min_d =12000;
        add = -1;
        for(int i =0; i<cnt; i++){
            if(V[i] == -1 && (i==s || v_
                min_d = D[i];
                add = i;
```

A for loop has a set number of times the loop should repeat.

15

A librarian could use loops to sort book titles.

Sometimes the coder does not know how many times an action should be repeated. In this case, coders can use *until* and *while* loops. An *until* loop repeats an action until there is nothing left to do. For example, a librarian wants a program to sort the titles of books in alphabetical order. But she does not know how many books the library carries. She uses an *until* loop to alphabetize each title until there are no more titles left to alphabetize.

While loops repeat tasks as long as the condition is true. For example, a *while* loop can tell a computer to do a task while it is a certain time of day. The computer will check the time as it completes each loop. When the time of day has passed, it will leave the loop.

Loops allow coders to only have to tell the computer how to do something once. This makes writing code easier and faster. Loops let the computer work hard so the coder does not have to.

English ▼

Elapsed Time: 00:03:09

Cancel

While *loops can make computers repeat tasks during certain times.*

Runn

Q: What happens if a loop does not have an increment?

  a. The computer will not start the loop.

  b. The computer will get stuck in the loop forever.

  c. The computer will only repeat the loop once.

  d. The loop will work normally.

A: b. The computer will get stuck in the loop forever.

Q: What are the four parts of a loop?

A: The four parts of a loop are the setup, condition, body, and increment.

Q: Why do coders use loops?

A: Coders use loops to make computers repeat actions with only one set of instructions.

Q: Which kind of loop is helpful if a coder does not know how many times the computer needs to repeat the loop?

    a. *for* loop

    b. *while* loop

    c. *until* loop

    d. Both b and c

A: d. Both b and c

GLOSSARY

body (BOD-ee) The body is the part of a loop that has the instructions for the computer to follow. The body of the loop made the computer write "Hello."

code (KOHD) Code is a list of instructions that computers follow to do things. The computer follows code that alphabetizes book titles.

coders (KOHD-urz) Coders are people who write code. Coders create computer programs.

condition (kun-DISH-uhn) A condition is something that is needed before a set of code can run. The condition must be true for the computer to enter a loop.

increment (IN-kre-ment) An increment is the part of a loop that keeps track of how many times the computer has repeated the loop. The increment told the computer that it had repeated the loop twice.

loop (LOOP) A loop is a type of code that tells a computer to repeat an action. The loop told the computer to type "Hello" 100 times.

setup (SET-up) The setup is the part of a loop that marks the beginning of a loop. The setup tells the computer what type of loop it is entering.

IN THE LIBRARY

Kulz, George Anthony. *How to Read Scratch Computer Code*. Mankato, MN: The Child's World, 2018.

Wood, Kevin. *Get Coding with Repeating*. New York, NY: Rosen Publishing, 2018.

Woolf, Alex. *You Wouldn't Want to Live without Coding!* New York, NY: Franklin Watts, 2019.

ON THE WEB

Visit our website for links about coding:
childsworld.com/links

Note to Parents, Teachers, and Librarians: We routinely verify our
Web links to make sure they are safe and active sites.
So encourage your readers to check them out!

INDEX